The Adventures of Layla

The Day Our Lives Changed Forever

Author: Lucreitia Usher
Co Authors: Layla and Jacob Dove

Illstrators: Megan Rizzo
Anita Hampton

Publisher: Breaking Barriers Publishing

Library of Congress Control Number: 2021922584
ISBN 9780578317670

Published and printed in the United States of America

LETTER FROM THE CO-AUTHORS

Hi, my name is Layla, and this is my brother Jacob. We wrote this book with our Mom to take you on a journey with us when the devastating virus, COVID-19, took over the world, impacting all of our lives. The day the world shut down will forever be a day we will never forget. We wanted to tell our story from a kid's perspective while adding our own twist of imagination and creativity. That day started off with celebrations and families spending time together and ended with a state of emergency and the beginning of a stay-at-home mandate. It was also the last day we were able to have any physical contact with our friends and families. For all students across the world, this was also the last day we were able to see our classmates and instantly had to adjust to our new norm of virtual interaction.

We dedicate this book to all frontline workers who worked countless hours, continuously dedicated to educating the community and keeping us safe. Our heart goes out to the millions of families who grieved the loss of their loved ones who were impacted by COVID-19. This pandemic will be part of our history, and the kids from our generation will always remember the year where we used technology to watch hours of social media challenges and stay connected with our families. We also won't forget the social isolation and virtual schooling. We want you to grab your families and sit together in your favorite place in your home. Take this book and read it together. Use this time to discuss how you felt when the world shut down. Talk about the lessons you learned during the pandemic.

Although we cannot change history, we can appreciate the much-needed time spent with family. Our Mom refers to 2021 as the "Year of the Reset." The year where everyone around the world had the opportunity to shift their focus in life and tap into their creative side. Did you discover your "special power?" The hidden talent you often put on hold because your time was limited before. Did your family create new traditions? Follow us on social media to share your new family traditions that were birthed during the pandemic.

From the bottom of our hearts, we hope you enjoy our book!

Happy Birthday Layla
8

Turning 8 is a VERY big deal to me. This birthday was very special; my Mom always told me the number 8 represents the number of creating new beginnings. She also told me that every birthday is a milestone that should be celebrated. My family and friends joined me for ice cream and cake; we sang happy birthday; I closed my eyes, made a wish and blew out the candles. I wished that I could travel to Florida for Christmas with my family and walk in the annual Christmas Day Parade. The entire day was filled with fun and games and lots of cake.

The next morning, I looked around my room and saw the leftover decorations scattered on the floor. I noticed a big purple box sitting next to a vintage mirror with a bow on it. I crawled out of my bed to open the box before school. To my surprise, inside was a purple shirt that my mom wore when she was my age and some fancy glitter boots. At the bottom of the box was a card that read:

"Happy Birthday, Princess! Another year around the sun and another opportunity for you to be celebrated by the people who love you. I'm so glad I get to continue our family tradition by passing down a letter from your great grandmother Carolyn and the vintage mirror that your grandmother Deborah had when she was your age. I know you're wondering why this birthday is so special; this letter will explain to you why turning 8 is so special in our family. Enjoy your gift!"

I grabbed the shirt out of the box and held it up to admire how great it would look. As I stared at the shirt, I remembered looking through an old photo album at my grandmother Deborah's house. I saw my Mom in the same shirt when she was 8 years old.

What does she mean the letter will explain why this birthday is so special? I thought. So many thoughts were running through my head, I got distracted and tossed the letter on the bed and continued admiring the shirt.

Suddenly, I heard a weird noise coming from the mirror. I paid it no mind and started getting dressed for school. A few minutes later, I could feel something strange behind me. Out of the corner of my eye, I noticed the mirror rocking and making weird noises. I turned slowly and noticed a strange glow coming from the mirror.

My heart started racing; I felt like my knees were getting weak. I didn't know if I should run or yell for my Mom, so I just sat on my bed and closed my eyes tightly, hoping when I opened them, this would stop. When I opened my eyes, the glow was gone, and I quickly put on the purple shirt and finished getting dressed for school.

I slowly tiptoed in front of the mirror to make sure it was clear to look. I stood in front of the mirror and noticed my reflection; I was shocked at what I saw. In my reflection, I was dressed up like a superhero. I tried not to scream; I grabbed my backpack and told my little brother, Jacob, to hurry up and eat his breakfast. After Jacob ate his breakfast, I told him to hurry and we ran out of the house to the bus stop.

The morning bus ride to school felt different. Normally on the way to school, Jacob and I would read comic books about superheroes who used their powers to fight off the bad guys and save the world.

We would use our 20-minute bus ride to imagine the day that our superpowers would be granted to us. We wanted to help save the world by fighting off bad guys. Although this morning started off weird, I remembered what my Mom said about the number 8. Maybe turning 8 really did mean something.

I sat on the bus quietly, listening to Jacob talk about our imaginary adventure of us flying across the world using our powers to fight off bad guys. I stared out the window and listened to him talk excitedly. I was not ready to tell him what happened to me this morning because our daily bus ride to school slowly turned into our comic book reality.

It was a normal afternoon at Clemens Elementary School. The sun was shining outside, and the hallways were filled with laughter. Recess was the highlight of our day; I couldn't wait to go outside and see Jacob and my best friend Aria. As time moved slow, I sat in class trying to figure out what really happened to me this morning. I had so many questions. Do I really have superpowers? Can I fly? Should I tell my parents?

My teacher, Ms. Jackie, told us we had five minutes before the bell rang. She then told us to draw a picture of what we wanted to be when we grew up for Show and Tell. As I started thinking of what to draw, I found myself thinking about this morning. I started drawing the vision I saw in the mirror of me as a superhero. I got so excited and realized this might not be a bad thing. I imagined myself being in a comic book and fighting off the bad guys with my sidekick, Jacob. My cape was made of glitter, and my boots lit up when I walked. My walk would be fierce, just like my favorite comic book character Madam K, I was empowered; I had Girl Power.

The bell rang and snapped me back to reality. I jumped up out of my seat and ran to the playground to eat my lunch. After I had eaten lunch, I saw Jacob playing football with his friends. Aria and I were hanging upside down on the monkey bars, trying not to barf up our lunch. The wind was blowing in my face, and we were both laughing and showing each other our gymnastic moves. I kept thinking to myself, *Am I really a superhero? Can I help save the world?*

I sat up on the monkey bars and looked up in the sky, praying it didn't rain on us.

Although the sun was shining, the sky started to get dark, and I said, "Something doesn't feel right." Suddenly, Ms. Elizabeth, our homeroom teacher, waved her arms in the air to signal for her class to come inside. That was strange because the bell hadn't rung yet. Then, I looked over at Ms. Jackie, who looked like she had seen a ghost. Aria and I climbed down from the monkey bars and quickly ran into the school.

As soon as we walked into school, I heard Principal Lamont on the loudspeaker announcing an emergency assembly being held in the gym. The hallway that led us to the gym was filled with chatter. The students at Clemens Elementary didn't look as worried as the teachers.

I looked for Jacob in the crowd and, when I found him, I asked how he was feeling. He told me he was scared and asked me if I knew what was going on. I told him I didn't know; we both sat on the gym floor and waited for Mr. Lamont's directions.

The excitement from recess had faded away, and every teacher looked worried. Principal Lamont told us that America had been hit with a "pandemic," and we had to leave school immediately to go home. He explained that it was a virus, and at this time we are not sure where the virus has come from, He told us we would be out of school until further notice.

The students were told that our parents would educate us more on what was going on. Every person in the room looked shocked, the silence in the room reminded me of how quiet Ms. Elizabeth wanted us to be in the library.

We were told to grab our belongings and meet our parents outside for pickup. We were told to stand by grade, with the Kindergartners going first.

The silence broke in the room, when Aria raised her hand and said, "Excuse me, Mr. Lamont, is the virus a mean person?" All the students started murmuring, confused by her questions. By the expression on our faces, we all had the same question. "No, Aria," Principal Lamont said, the virus is not a person. The virus is a very powerful germ called Covid-19 that can cause you to be very sick. He grabbed the mic on the podium, and his deep voice started to tremble. He was lost for words and told us our parents would explain the virus to us in more detail when we got home.

When our Mom came to pick us up, we got in the car, sad and confused. Mom was quiet at first like she was trying to find the exact words to say. With everything going on, Mom didn't notice that I was wearing her old shirt. I also couldn't talk to her about what happened to me this morning.

While driving home, she told Jacob and I about the virus called "COVID-19." She said that it had taken over the world and was extremely dangerous. She heard on the news that the virus can make us really sick. She said that, for now, kids weren't really getting sick. But the virus was mostly attacking adults. She also said that the whole world was now on lockdown until further notice.

We were told that all schools were closed, and we wouldn't be able to visit our family and friends for a while. Mom was told by the principal that our teachers would email her the plan for finishing the rest of the school year. They would also tell all parents how we could stay connected with our classmates.

During the silent drive home, I was confused, scared, and worried about what was going on in the world. I know I'm only 8, but I still have a lot of questions; this was a lot for any kids to take in.

That evening, we all sat on the floor in our family room, watching the local news. The news reporter, Pat Brown, was covering news on the virus and warned all Michigan residents to stay at home.

While sitting on the floor in silence, Mom yelled at the TV, "Toilet paper!" As the excitement in her voice startled us, we all started laughing. Her outburst broke the silence. My older brother, Jamir, asked why there was a toilet paper shortage and Mom explained that all of America is currently panicking and there is a shortage of toilet paper, food, water, and disinfectant supplies.

Mom also told us that Governor Gretch had advised all Michigan residents to wear a mask, gloves, and a face shield to prevent the spread of the virus. Mom scratched her head in disbelief and said in a soft tone, "This cannot be our new normal."I went upstairs and sat on the floor of my room in disbelief. I am only 8 years old; this is too much to handle. Today was so overwhelming; How did America get here? I wondered. The tears wouldn't stop falling, and I found myself thinking about how kids around the World were feeling. With what happened this morning, I might be able to save all the families in the World.

I needed something to cheer me up, so I grabbed the letter my great-grandmother wrote and sat on the floor to read it out loud.

"The Family Affirmation"

You will be an amazing young lady who will be filled with wisdom and knowledge that was passed down from your lineage. You are brilliant and stronger than you think. You will be an inquisitive and mighty warrior. Inside of the mirror is a cape that I made with your grandmother Deborah when you were a baby. When you put the cape on, your powers will be activated. Your heart is your superpower, and you will use it to touch millions of people. The mirror is to remind you to love the skin you are in. The glow from the mirror will ensure that you always light up a room. Always remember who you are and your connection to strong women. I know turning 8 is a big deal in our family, but you deserve to wear this cape that symbolizes strength and love. I know one day you will be a great example for your generation.

I was trying to fight back the tears while reading the letter. It was such an honor to read a letter that was handwritten by my great grandmother. My mother always wanted to keep the legacy of my great-grandmothers alive. She speaks very highly about them and how much of an impact they made on her life.

I slowly wiped the tears, opened the mirror, and wiped off the box filled with dust. I opened the box and put on the cape. I grabbed my matching glitter boots out of the closet and stood in front of the mirror. I began to smile in excitement, and I started reciting the words of affirmation in my head, and I instantly felt empowered.

Suddenly, the floor started shaking, and the mirror started rocking. My cape and boots were glowing, and my purple shirt had a heart in the center. The glow from the room made Jacob burst in, his face filled with surprise.

"Layla is that you?!"

"Yes!" I screamed.

"What's going on?" he asked.

"Sit down and let me explain."

So, I told him what had happened to me earlier that day. He was shocked and then asked me what my superhero name was and do I have special powers. I told him that many years ago, our great-grandmother named me a mighty warrior, and the heart on my chest symbolizes the love I have for the world.

I told him my job is to do everything in love by educating, protecting, and saving children from this mean virus.

Jacob was so surprised and glowed with excitement. "How do you plan to save the world?"

First, we are going to make masks for all students at Clemens Elementary," I stated. "Then, we are going to deliver them to the families. Jacob was so excited to help me he anxiously grabbed my hand and told me we needed to get started. Before we left my room, I told Jacob he had to keep my superpowers a secret. The time will come when I will share my powers with our family first and then the world. We did our special handshake, and Jacob promised me he wouldn't tell mom or my big brother Jamir.

I couldn't believe what was happening; it was all making sense now the reflection I saw this morning was real. I am a superhero with my own special powers. What if I can fight off the virus and keep my friends and family safe?

Jacob ran out of my room and told me he would grab his supplies to help make the mask. I told him, ok and started looking for my crafting supplies as well. I remember hearing Pat Brown, the reporter, say that wearing a mask and gloves when going outside will help us stay protected from the virus. She mentioned something about "PPE," so

I grabbed my tablet and googled what that was. It turns out that it stands for "Personal Protective Equipment."

I quickly went into my toy chest and grabbed an old rag and some gloves I had from an old costume. I then googled what a mask looked like and went into my Mom's crafting room to try and sew a mask. I took a sewing class with my Girl Scouts Troop, so I remembered the basics.

Once I was done, I put the mask and gloves on. Now I have the missing pieces to my costume! I looked in the mirror and was ready to fight off the mean virus.

Before going to get the rest of my family to meet in Mom's crafting room to help make the mask. I took off my costume and put it in the back of my closet. Jacob and I promised we would keep this secret between us both. I wanted to focus on making the mask for the students of Clemens Elementary.

That night we joined together as a family in Mom's craft room and discussed what happened that day. I sat on the floor with my Mom and helped both of my brothers design and make a mask.

I thought about all the events that day. First, I woke up and found out I was a superhero. According to the letter I read, I have special powers that were passed down from my great-grandmother. Then, students at my school were sent home because of a virus that had taken over the world. What the world once thought was normal had changed unexpectedly in a blink of an eye.

I can't see my friends and family anymore; hugs are banned until further notice. Schools are closed, and I heard my grandmother Deborah say we have to finish school virtually.

Not to mention the shortage of food, water, disinfectants supplies, and toilet paper, This has been a long day! The news said the pandemic would be part of history, and we will never forget this day because it changed our lives.

At the age of 8, this was a lot for me to understand. I could only imagine how my brothers and other kids across the world were feeling.

We have no clue what tomorrow brings but sitting in this room makes me look at my family and appreciate the love that we have for each other. We all sat on the floor, our Mom grabbing us close and hugging us tightly.

All at once, we said, "We are all in this together."

WE HOPE YOU ENJOYED THE BOOK!
PLEASE TAKE A PICTURE WITH YOUR FAMILY HOLDING THE BOOK AND TAG US ON INSTAGRAM.

BREAKING_BARRIERS__FAMILY

Made in the USA
Monee, IL
07 November 2021

81575686R00024